The Lady in the Van

The Lady in
the Van

*

Alan Bennett

London Review of Books

1990

The Lady in the Van was first published in the *London Review of Books* in 1989

Published by LRB Limited
Tavistock House South, Tavistock Square
London WC1H 9JZ

First published 1990
Copyright © Alan Bennett 1989

Printed in England by Expression Printers, London

ISBN 1 873092 00 8

'I ran into a snake this afternoon,' Miss Shepherd said. 'It was coming up Parkway. It was a long, grey snake, a boa constrictor possibly, it looked poisonous. It was keeping close to the wall and seemed to know its way. I've a feeling it may have been heading for the van.' I was relieved that on this occasion she didn't demand that I ring the police, as she regularly did if anything out of the ordinary occurred. Perhaps this was too out of the ordinary (though it turned out the pet shop in Parkway had been broken into the previous night, so she may have seen a snake). She brought her mug over and I made her a drink which she took back to the van. 'I thought I'd better tell you,' she said, 'just to be on the safe side. I've had some close shaves with snakes.'

This encounter with the putative boa constrictor was in the summer of 1971 when Miss Shepherd and her van had for some months been at a permanent halt opposite my house in Camden Town. I had first come across her a few years previously, stood by her van, stalled as usual, near the convent at the top of the street. The convent (which was to have a subsequent career as the Japanese School) was a gaunt reformatory-like building that housed a dwindling garrison of aged nuns and was notable for a striking crucifix attached to the wall overlooking the traffic lights. There was something about the position of Christ, pressing himself against the grim pebbledash beneath the barred windows of the convent, that called up visions of the Stalag and the searchlight and which had caused us to dub him 'The Christ of Colditz'. Miss Shepherd, not looking un-crucified herself, was standing by her vehicle in an attitude with which I was to

5

become very familiar, left arm extended with the palm flat against the side of the van indicating ownership, the right arm summoning anyone who was fool enough to take notice of her, on this occasion me. Nearly six foot, she was a commanding figure and would have been more so had she not been kitted out in greasy raincoat, orange skirt, Ben Hogan golfing cap and carpet slippers. She would be going on sixty at this time.

She must have prevailed on me to push the van as far as Albany Street, though I recall nothing of the exchange. What I do remember was being overtaken by two policemen in a panda car as I trundled the van across Gloucester Bridge; I thought that, as the van was certainly holding up the traffic, they might have lent a hand. They were wiser than I knew. The other feature of this first run-in with Miss Shepherd was her driving technique. Scarcely had I put my shoulder to the back of the van, an old Bedford, than a long arm was stretched elegantly out of the driver's window to indicate in textbook fashion that she (or rather I) was moving off. A few yards further on, as we were about to turn into Albany Street, the arm emerged again, twirling elaborately in the air to indicate that we were branching left, the movement done with such boneless grace that this section of the Highway Code might have been choreographed by Petipa with Ulanova at the wheel. Her 'I am coming to a halt' was less poised, as she had plainly not expected me to give up pushing and shouted angrily back that it was the other end of Albany Street she wanted, a mile further on. But I had had enough by this time and left her there with no thanks for my trouble. Far from it. She even climbed out of the van and came running after me, shouting that I had no business abandoning her, so that passers-by looked at me as if I had done some injury to this

6

pathetic scarecrow. 'Some people!' I suppose I thought, feeling foolish that I'd been taken for a ride (or taken her for one) and cross that I'd fared worse than if I'd never lifted a finger, these mixed feelings to be the invariable aftermath of any transaction involving Miss Shepherd. One seldom was able to do her a good turn without some thoughts of strangulation.

It must have been a year or so after this, and so some time in the late Sixties, that the van first appeared in Gloucester Crescent. In those days the street was still a bit of a mixture. Its large semi-detached villas had originally been built to house the Victorian middle class, then it had gone down in the world, and though it had never entirely decayed, many of the villas degenerated into rooming-houses and so were among the earliest candidates for what is now called 'gentrification', but which was then called 'knocking through'. Young professional couples, many of them in journalism or television, bought up the houses, converted them and (an invariable feature of such conversions) knocked the basement rooms together to form a large kitchen-dining-room. In the mid-Sixties I wrote a BBC TV series, *Life in NW1*, based on one such family, the Stringalongs, whom Mark Boxer then took over to people a cartoon strip in the *Listener*, and who kept cropping up in his drawings for the rest of his life. What made the social set-up funny was the disparity between the style in which the new arrivals found themselves able to live and their progressive opinions: guilt, put simply, which today's gentrifiers are said famously not to feel (or 'not to have a problem about'). We did have a problem, though I'm not sure we were any better for it. There was a gap between our social position and our social obligations. It was in this gap that Miss Shepherd (in her van) was able to live.

7

October 1969 When she is not in the van Miss S. spends much of her day sitting on the pavement in Parkway, where she has a pitch outside Williams and Glyn's Bank. She sells tracts, entitled 'True View: Mattering Things', which she writes herself though this isn't something she will admit. 'I sell them but so far as the authorship is concerned, I'll say they are anonymous and that's as far as I'm prepared to go.' She generally chalks the gist of the current pamphlet on the pavement, though with no attempt at artistry. 'St Francis FLUNG money from him' is today's message and prospective customers have to step over it to get into the bank. She also makes a few coppers selling pencils. 'A gentleman came the other day and said that the pencil he had bought from me was the best pencil on the market at the present time. It lasted him three months. He'll be back for another one shortly.' D., one of the more conventional neighbours (and not a Knocker-Through), stops me and says: 'Tell me, is she a *genuine* eccentric?'

April 1970 Today we moved the old lady's van. An obstruction order has been put under the windscreen wiper, stating that it was stationed outside No 63 and is a danger to public health. This order, Miss S. insists, is a statutory order: 'And statutory means standing, in this case standing outside No 63, so if the van is moved on, the order will be invalid.' Nobody ventures to argue with this but she can't decide whether her next pitch should be outside No 61 or further on. Eventually she decides there is 'a nice space' outside 62 and plumps for that. Nick Tomalin and I heave away at the back of the van but while she is gracefully indicating that she is moving off (for all of the fifteen feet) the van doesn't budge. 'Have you let the handbrake off?' Nick

Tomalin asks. There is a pause. 'I'm just in the process of taking it off.' As we are poised for the move, another Camden Town eccentric materialises, a tall elderly figure in long overcoat and Homburg hat, with a distinguished grey moustache and in his buttonhole a flag for the Primrose League. He takes off a grubby canary glove and leans a shaking hand against the rear of the van (OLU 246), and when we have moved it forward the few statutory feet, he puts on his glove again, saying: 'If you should need me I'm just round the corner' (i.e. in Arlington House). I ask Miss S. how long she has had the van. 'Since 1965,' she says, 'though don't spread that around. I got it to put my things in. I came down from St Albans in it and plan to go back there eventually. I'm just pedalling water at the moment. I've always been in the transport line. Chiefly delivery and chauffeuring. You know,' she says mysteriously, 'renovated army vehicles. And I've got good topography. I always have had. I knew Kensington in the black-out.'

This van (there were to be three others in the course of the next twenty years) was originally brown but by the time it had reached the Crescent it had been given a coat of yellow. Miss S. was fond of yellow ('It's the Papal colour') and was never content to leave her vehicles long in their original trim. Sooner or later she could be seen moving slowly round her immobile home, thoughtfully touching up the rust from a tiny tin of primrose paint, looking, in her long dress and sun hat, much as Vanessa Bell would have looked had she gone in for painting Bedford vans. Miss S. never appreciated the difference between car enamel and ordinary gloss paint and even this she never bothered to mix. The result was that all her vehicles ended up looking as

9

if they had been given a coat of badly-made custard or plastered with scrambled egg. Still, there were few occasions on which one saw Miss Shepherd genuinely happy and one of them was when she was putting paint on. A few years before she died she went in for a Reliant Robin (to put more of her things in). It was actually yellow to start with, but that didn't save it from an additional coat which she applied as Monet might have done, standing back to judge the effect of each brush-stroke. The Reliant stood outside my gate. It was towed away earlier this year, a scatter of yellow drops on the kerb all that remains to mark its final parking place.

January 1971 Charity in Gloucester Crescent takes refined forms. The publishers next door are bringing out some Classical volume and to celebrate the event last night held a Roman Dinner. This morning the au pair was to be seen knocking at the window of the van with a plate of Roman remains. But Miss S. is never easy to help. After 12 last night I saw her striding up the Crescent waving her stick and telling someone to be off. Then I heard a retreating middle-class voice say plaintively: 'But I only asked if you were all right.'

June 1971 Scarcely a day passes now without some sort of incident involving the old lady. Yesterday evening around ten a sports car swerves over to her side of the road so that the driver, rich, smart and in his twenties, can lean over and bang on the side of the van, presumably to flush out for his grinning girlfriend the old witch who lives there. I shout at him and he sounds his horn and roars off. Miss S. of course wants the police called, but I can't see the point and indeed around five this morning I wake to find

10

two policemen at much the same game, idly shining their torches in the windows in the hope that she'll wake up and enliven a dull hour of their beat. Tonight a white car reverses dramatically up the street, screeches to a halt beside the van and a burly young man jumps out and gives the van a terrific shaking. Assuming (hoping, probably) he would have driven off by the time I get outside, I find he's still there, and ask him what the fuck he thinks he's doing. His response is quite mild. 'What's up with you then?' he asks. 'You still on the telly? You nervous? You're trembling all over.' He then calls me a fucking cunt and drives off. After all that, of course, Miss S. isn't in the van at all, so I end up as usual more furious with her than I am with the lout.

These attacks, I'm sure, disturbed my peace of mind more than they did hers. Living in the way she did every day must have brought such cruelties. Some of the stallholders in the Inverness Street market used to persecute her with Medieval relish – and children too, who both inflict and suffer such casual cruelties themselves. One night two drunks systematically smashed all the windows of the van, the flying glass cutting her face. Furious over any small liberty, she was only mildly disturbed by this. 'They may have had too much to drink by mistake,' she says, 'that does occur through not having eaten, possibly. I don't want a case.' She's far more interested in 'a ginger feller I saw in Parkway in company with Mr Khrushchev. Has he disappeared recently?'

But to find such sadism and intolerance so close at hand began actively to depress me and having to be on the alert for every senseless attack made it impossible to work. There came a day when after a long succession of such incidents I suggested that

11

she spend at least the nights in a lean-to at the side of my house. Initially reluctant, as with any change, over the next two years she gradually abandoned the van for the hut.

In giving her sanctuary in my garden and landing myself with a tenancy that went on eventually for fifteen years I was never under any illusion that the impulse was purely charitable. And of course it made me furious that I had been driven to such a pass. But I wanted a quiet life as much as, and possibly more than, she did. In the garden she was at least out of harm's way.

October 1973 I have run a lead out to the lean-to and now regularly have to mend Miss S.'s electric fire which she keeps fusing by plugging too many appliances into the attachment. I sit on the steps fiddling with the fuse while she squats on her haunches in the hut. 'Aren't you cold? You could come in here. I could light a candle and then it would be a bit warmer. The toad's been in once or twice. He was in here with a slug. I think he may be in love with the slug. I tried to turn it out and it got very disturbed. I thought he was going to go for me.' She complains that there is not enough room in the shed and suggests I get her a tent which she could then use to store some of her things. 'It would only be three feet high and by rights ought to be erected in a meadow. Then there are these shatterproof greenhouses. Or something could be done with old raincoats possibly.'

March 1974 The Council are introducing parking restrictions in the Crescent. Residents' bays have been provided and yellow lines drawn up the rest of the street. To begin with, the workmen are very understanding, painting the yellow line as far as the van, then beginning again on the other side so that technically it is still legally parked. However, a higher official has now stepped in and served a removal order on it, so all this week there has been a great deal of activity as Miss S. transports cargoes of plastic bags across the road, through the garden and into the hut. While professing faith in divine protection for the van, she is prudently clearing out her belongings against its possible removal. A notice she has written declaring the Council's action illegal twirls idly under the windscreen wiper. 'The notice was served on a Sunday. I believe you can serve search warrants on a Sunday but nothing else, possibly. I should have the Freedom of the Land for the good articles I've sold on the economy.' She is particularly concerned about the tyres of the van which 'may be miraculous. They've only been pumped up twice since 1964. If I get another vehicle' – and Lady W. is threatening to buy her one – 'I'd like them transferred.'

The old van was towed away in April 1974 and another one provided by Lady W. ('a titled Catholic lady', as Miss S. always referred to her). Happy to run to a new (albeit old) van, Lady W. was understandably not anxious to have it parked outside her front door and eventually, and perhaps by now inevitably, the van and Miss S. ended up in my garden. This van was roadworthy and Miss S. insisted on being the one to drive it through the gate into the garden, a manoeuvre which once again enabled her to go through her full repertoire of hand signals. Once the van was on site Miss S. applied the handbrake with such determination that like Excalibur it could never thereafter be released, rusting so firmly into place that when the van came to be moved ten years later it had to be hoisted over the wall by the council crane.

This van (and its successor, bought in 1983) now occupied a paved area between my front door and the garden gate, the bonnet of the van hard by my front step, its rear door, which Miss S. always used to get in and out of, a few feet from the gate. Callers at the house had to squeeze past the back of the van and come down the side and while they waited for my door to be opened they would be scrutinised from behind the murky windscreen by Miss Shepherd. If they were unlucky, they would find the rear door open with Miss S. dangling her large white legs over the back. The interior of the van, a midden of old clothes, plastic bags and half-eaten food, was not easy to ignore but should anyone Miss S. did not know venture to speak to her she would promptly tuck her legs back and wordlessly shut the door. For the first few years of her sojourn in the garden I would try and explain to mystified callers how this situation had arisen, but after a while I ceased to care and when I didn't mention it nor did anyone else.

At night the impression was haunting. I had run a cable out from the house to give her light and heating and through the ragged draperies that hung over the windows of the van a visitor would glimpse Miss S.'s spectral figure, often bent over in prayer or lying on her side like an effigy on a tomb, her face resting on one hand, listening to Radio 4. Did she hear any movement she would straightaway switch off the light and wait like an animal that has been disturbed until she was sure the coast was clear and could put the light on again. She retired early and would complain if anyone called or left late at night. On one occasion Coral Browne was coming away from the house with her husband, Vincent Price, and they were talking quietly. 'Pipe down,' snapped the voice from the van, 'I'm trying to sleep.' For someone

14

who had brought terror to millions it was an unexpected taste of his own medicine.

December 1974 Miss S. has been explaining to me why the old Bedford (the van not the music-hall) ceased to go 'possibly'. She had put in some of her home-made petrol, based on a recipe for petrol substitute she read about several years ago in a newspaper. 'It was a spoonful of petrol, a gallon of water and a pinch of something you could get in every High Street. Well, I got it into my head, I don't know why, that it was bicarbonate of soda, only I think I was mistaken. It must be either sodium chloride or sodium nitrate, only I've since been told sodium chloride is salt and the man in Boots wouldn't sell me the other, saying it might cause explosions. Though I think me being an older person he knew I would be more responsible. Though not all old ladies perhaps.'

February 1975 Miss S. rings and when I open the door she makes a bee-line for the kitchen stairs. 'I'd like to see you. I've called several times. I wonder whether I can use the toilet first.' I say I think this is pushing it a bit. 'I'm not pushing it at all. I just will do the interview better if I can use the toilet first.' Afterwards she sits down in her green mac and purple headscarf, the knuckles of one large mottled hand resting on the clean scrubbed table, and explains how she has devised a method of 'getting on the wireless'. I was to ask the BBC to give me a phone-in programme ('something someone like you could get put on in a jiffy') and then she would ring me up from the house. 'Either that or I could get on *Petticoat Line*. I know a darn sight more on moral matters than most of them. I could sing my song over the telephone. It's

15

a lovely song, called "The End of the World".' (Which is pure *Beyond the Fringe*.) 'I won't commit myself to singing it, not at this moment, but I probably would. Some sense should be said and knowledge known. It could all be anonymous. I could be called The Lady Behind the Curtain. Or A Woman of Britain. You could take a nom-de-plume view of it.' This idea of The Woman Behind the Curtain has obviously taken her fancy and she begins to expand on it, demonstrating where the curtain could be, her side of it coincidentally taking in the television and the easy chair. She could be behind the curtain, she explains, do her periodic broadcasts and the rest of the time 'be a guest at the television and take in some civilisation. Perhaps there could be gaps filled with nice classical music. I know one: Prelude and "Liebestraum" by Liszt. I believe he was a Catholic priest. It means "love's dream", only not the sexy stuff. It's the love of God and the sanctification of labour and so on, which would recommend it to celibates like you and me, possibly.' Shocked at this tentative bracketing of our conditions, I quickly get rid of her and, though it's a bitter cold night, open the windows wide to get rid of the smell.

The Women Behind the Curtain remained a favourite project of hers and in 1976 she wrote to Aiman (*sic*) Andrews: 'Now that *This is your life* is ended, having cost too much etc, I might be able to do a bit as The Lady Behind the Curtain. All you need do is put a curtain up to hide me but permit words of sense to come forth in answer to some questions. Sense is needed.' Hygiene was needed too, but possibly in an effort to persuade me about being behind the curtain she brought the subject up herself: 'I'm by nature a very clean person. I have a testimonial for a Clean Room, awarded me some years ago and my aunt, herself spotless, said I was the cleanest of my mother's children particularly in the unseen places.' I never fathomed her toilet arrangements. She only once asked me to buy her toilet rolls ('I use them to wipe my face'), but whatever happened in that department I took to be part of some complicated arrangement involving the plastic bags she used to hurl from the van every morning. When she could still manage stairs she did very occasionally use my loo but I didn't encourage it; it was here on the threshold of the toilet that my charity stopped short. Once when I was having some building work done (and was, I suppose, conscious of what the workmen were thinking), I very boldly said there was a smell of urine. 'Well, what can you expect when they're raining bricks down on me all day? And then I think there's a mouse. So that would make a cheesy smell, possibly.'

Miss S.'s daily emergence from the van was highly dramatic. Suddenly and without warning the rear door would be flung open to reveal the tattered draperies that masked the terrible interior. There was a pause, then through the veils would be hurled several bulging plastic sacks. Another pause, before slowly and with great caution one sturdy slippered leg came feeling for the floor before the other followed and one had the first sight of the day's wardrobe. Hats were always a feature: a black railwayman's hat with a long neb worn slightly on the skew so that she looked like a drunken signalman or a French guardsman of the 1880s; there was her Charlie Brown pitcher's hat; and in June 1977 an octagonal straw table mat, tied on with a chiffon scarf and a bit of cardboard for the peak. She also went in for green eyeshades. Her skirts had a telescopic appearance as they had

17

often been lengthened many times over by the simple expedient of sewing a strip of extra cloth around the hem, though with no attempt at matching. One skirt was made by sewing several orange dusters together. When she fell foul of authority she put it down to her clothes. Once late at night the police rang me from Tunbridge Wells. They had picked her up on the station, thinking her dress was a nighty. She was indignant. 'Does it look like a nighty? You see lots of people wearing dresses like this. I don't think this style can have got to Tunbridge Wells yet.'

Miss S. seldom wore stockings and alternated between black pumps and brown carpet slippers. Her hands and feet were large and she was what my grandmother would have called 'a big-boned woman'. She was middle-class and spoke in a middle-class way, though her querulous and often resentful demeanour tended to obscure this; it wasn't a gentle or a genteel voice. Running through her vocabulary was a streak of schoolgirl slang. She wouldn't say she was tired, she was 'all done up'; petrol was 'juice' and if she wasn't keen on doing something she'd say 'I'm darned if I will.' All her conversation was impregnated with the vocabulary of her peculiar brand of Catholic fanaticism ('the dire importance of justice deeds'). It was the language of the leaflets she wrote, the 'possibly' with which she ended so many of her sentences an echo of the 'Subject to the Roman Catholic Church in her rights etc' with which she headed every leaflet.

May 1976 I have had some manure delivered for the garden and since the manure heap is not far from the van, Miss S. is concerned that people passing might think the smell is coming from there. She wants me to put a notice on the gate to the effect that the smell is the manure not her. I say no, without adding, as I could, that the manure actually smells much nicer. I am working in the garden when Miss B., the social worker, comes with a boxful of clothes. Miss S. is reluctant to open the van door as she is listening to *Any answers*, but eventually she slides on her bottom to the door of the van and examines the clothes. She is unimpressed.

Miss S.: I only asked for one coat.

Miss B.: Well, I brought three just in case you wanted a change.

Miss S. : I haven't got room for three. Besides, I was planning to wash this coat in the near-future. That makes four.

Miss B.: This is my old nursing mac.

Miss S.: I have a mac. Besides, green doesn't suit me. Have you got the stick?

Miss B.: No. That's being sent down. It had to be made specially.

Miss S.: Will it be long enough?

Miss B.: Yes. It's a special stick.

Miss S.: I don't want a special stick. I want an ordinary stick. Only longer. Does it have a rubber thing on it?

When Miss B. has gone Miss S. sits at the door of the van slowly turning over the contents of the box like a chimpanzee, sniffing them and holding them up and muttering to herself.

June 1976 I am sitting on the steps mending my bike when Miss S. emerges for her evening stroll. 'I went to Devon on Saturday,' she said. 'On this frisbee.' I suppose she means freebee, a countrywide concession to pensioners that BR ran last weekend. 'Dawlish I went to. People very nice. The man over the loud-speaker called us Ladies and Gentlemen, and so he should.

19

There was one person shouted, only he wasn't one of us, the son of somebody I think.' And almost for the first time ever she smiled, and said how they had all been bunched up trying to get into this one carriage, a great crowd, and how she had been hoisted up. 'It would have made a film,' she said. 'I thought of you.' And she stands there in her grimy raincoat, strands of lank grey hair escaping from under her headscarf. I am thankful people had been nice to her and wonder what the carriage must have been like all that hot afternoon. She then tells me about a programme on Francis Thompson she'd heard on the wireless, how he had tried to become a priest but had felt he had failed in his vocation, and had become a tramp. Then, unusually, she told me a little of her own life, and how she tried to become a nun on two occasions, had undergone instruction as a novice but was forced to give it up on account of ill-health, and that she had felt for many years that she had failed. But that this was wrong, and it was not a failure. 'If I could have had more modern clothes, longer sleep and better air, possibly, I would have made it.'

'A bit of a spree,' she called her trip to Dawlish. 'My spree.'

June 1977 On this the day of the Jubilee Miss S. has stuck a paper Union Jack in the cracked back window of the van. It is the only one in the Crescent. Yesterday she was wearing a headscarf and pinned across the front of it a blue Spontex sponge fastened at each side with a large safety pin, the sponge meant to form some kind of peak against the (very watery) sun. It looked like a favour worn by a Medieval knight or a fillet to ward off evil spirits. Still, it's better than last week's effort, an Afrika Korps cap from Lawrence Corner: Miss Shepherd – Desert Fox.

September 1979 Miss S. shows me a photograph she has taken of herself in a cubicle at Waterloo. She is very low in the frame, her mouth pulled down, the photo looking as if it has been taken after death. She is very pleased with it. 'I don't take a good photograph usually. That's the only photograph I've seen looks anything like me.' She wants two copies making of it. I say that it would be easier for her to go back to Waterloo and do two more. No. That would 'take it out of her'. 'I had one taken in France once when I was 21 or 22. Had to go into the next village for it. I came out cross-eyed. I saw someone else's photo on their bus-pass and she'd come out looking like a nigger. You don't want to come out like a nigger if you can help it, do you?'

June 1980 Miss S. has gone into her summer rig: a raincoat turned inside out with brown canvas panels and a large label declaring it the Emerald Weatherproof. This is topped off with a lavender chiffon scarf tied round a sun visor made from an old cornflakes packet. She asks me to do her some shopping. 'I want a small packet of Eno's, some milk and some jelly babies. The jelly babies aren't urgent. Oh and Mr Bennett. Could you get me one of those little bottles of whisky. I believe Bell's is very good. I don't drink it. I just use it to rub on.'

August 1980 I am filming and Miss S. sees me leaving early each morning and returning late. Tonight her scrawny hand comes out with a letter marked 'Please consider carefully':

An easier way for Mr Bennett to earn could be possibly with my co-operative part. Two young men could follow me in a car, one with a camera to get a funny film like 'Old Mother Riley Joins Up' possibly. If the car stalls they could then push it. Or they could go on the buses with her at a distance. Comedy happens without trying sometimes, or at least an interesting film covering a Senior Citizen's use of the buses can occur. One day to Hounslow, another to Reading or Heathrow. The bus people ought to be pleased, but it might need their permission. Then Mr Bennett could put his feet up more and rake it in, possibly.

October 1980 Miss S. has started hankering after a caravan trailer and has just missed one she saw in *Exchange and Mart*: 'little net curtains all round, three bunks'. 'I wouldn't use them all, except,' she says ominously, 'to put things on. Nice little windows – £275. They said it was sold only they may have thought I was just an old tramp . . . I was thinking of offering to help Mrs Thatcher with the economy. I wouldn't ask any money as I'm on social security, so it would come cheap for her. I might ask her for some perks though. Like a caravan. I would write to her but she's away. I know what's required. It's perfectly simple: justice.'

No political party quite catered to Miss S.'s views, though the National Front came close. She was passionately anti-Communist and as long ago as 1945 had written a letter to Jesus 'concerning the dreadful situation feared from the Yalta agreement'. The trouble was that her political opinions, while never moderate, were always tempered by her idiosyncratic view of the human physiognomy. Older was invariably wiser, which is fair if debatable, except that with Miss S. taller was wiser too. But height had its drawbacks and it was perhaps because she was tall herself that she believed a person's height added to their burdens, put them under some strain. Hence, though she was in sympathy with Mr Heath on everything except the Common Market, 'I do think that Mr Wilson, personally, may have seen

22

better in regard to Europe being on the opposition bench with less salary and being older, smaller and under less strain.' She was vehemently opposed to the Common Market, the 'common' always underlined when she wrote about it on the pavement as if it were the sheer vulgarity of the economic union she particularly objected to. Never very lucid in her leaflets, she got especially confused over the EEC. 'Not long ago a soul wrote, or else was considering writing (she cannot recall as to which and it may have been something of either) that she disassociated from the Common Market entry and the injustices feared concerning it, or something like that.' 'Enoch', as she invariably called Mr Powell, had got it right and she wrote him several letters telling him so, but in the absence of a wholly congenial party she founded her own, the Fidelis Party. 'It will be a party caring for Justice (and as such not needing opposition). Justice in the world today with its gigantic ignorant conduct requires the rule of a Good Dictator, possibly.'

Miss S. never regarded herself as being at the bottom of the social heap. That place was occupied by 'the desperate poor' – i.e. those with no roof over their heads. She herself was 'a cut above those in dire need' and one of her responsibilities in society she saw as interceding for them and for those whose plight she thought Mrs Thatcher had overlooked. Could it be brought to her attention (and she wrote Mrs T. several letters on the subject) alleviation would surely follow.

Occasionally she would write letters to other public figures. In August 1978 it was to the College of Cardinals, then busy electing a Pope. 'Your Eminences. I would like to suggest humbly that an older Pope might be admirable. Height can count towards knowledge too probably.' However this older (and hopefully taller) Pope she was recommending might find the ceremony a bit of a trial so, ever the expert on headgear, she suggests that 'at the Coronation there could be a not so heavy crown, of light plastic possibly or cardboard for instance.'

February 1981 Miss S. has flu so I am doing her shopping. I wait every morning by the side window of the van and, with the dark interior and her grimy hand holding back the tattered purple curtain, it is as if I am at the Confessional. The chief items this morning were ginger nuts ('very warming') and grape juice. 'I think this is what they must have been drinking at Cana,' she says as I hand her the bottle. 'Jesus wouldn't have wanted them rolling about drunk and this is non-alcoholic. It wouldn't do for everyone but in my opinion it's better than champagne.'

October 1981 The curtain is drawn aside this morning and Miss S. still in what I take to be her nightclothes talks of 'the discernment of spirits' that enabled her to sense an angelic presence near her when she was ill. At an earlier period, when she had her pitch outside the bank, she had sensed a similar angelic presence and now, having seen his campaign leaflet, who should this turn out to be, 'possibly', but Our Conservative Candidate Mr Pasley-Tyler. She embarks on a long disquisition on her well-worn theme of age-in politics. Mrs Thatcher is too young and travels too much. Not like President Reagan. 'You wouldn't catch him making all those U-turns round Australia.'

January 1982 'Do you see he's been found, that American soldier?' This is Colonel Dozo, kidnapped by the Red Brigade and found after a shoot-out in a flat in Padua. 'Yes, he's been found,'

24

she says triumphantly, 'and I know who found him.' Thinking it unlikely she has an acquaintance in the Italian version of the SAS, I ask whom she means. 'St Anthony of course. The patron saint of lost things. St Anthony of Padua.' 'Well,' I want to say, 'he didn't have far to look.'

May 1982 As I am leaving for Yorkshire Miss S.'s hand comes out like the Ancient Mariner's: do I know if there are any steps at Leeds Station? 'Why?' I ask warily, thinking she may be having thoughts of camping on my other doorstep. It turns out she just wants somewhere to go for a ride, so I suggest Bristol. 'Yes, I've been to Bristol. On the way back I came through Bath. That looked nice. Some beautifully parked cars.' She then recalls driving her reconditioned Army vehicles and taking them up to Derbyshire. 'I did it in the war,' she says. 'Actually I overdid it in the war,' and somehow that is the thin end of the wedge that has landed her up here, yearning for travel on this May morning forty years later.

'Land' is a word Miss S. prefers to 'country'. 'This land'. Used in this sense, it's part of the rhetoric, if not of madness at any rate of obsession. Jehovah's Witnesses talk of 'this land' and the National Front. Land is country plus destiny, country in the sight of God. Mrs Thatcher talks of 'this land'.

February 1983 A. telephones me in Yorkshire to say that the basement is under three inches of water, the boiler having burst. When told that the basement has been flooded, Miss S.'s only comment is: 'What a waste of water.'

April 1983 'I've been having bad nights,' says Miss S., 'but if I were elected I might have better nights.' She wants me to get her nomination papers so that she can stand for Parliament in the coming election. She would be the Fidelis Party candidate. The party, never very numerous, is now considerably reduced. Once she could count on five votes but now there are only two, one of whom is me, and I don't like to tell her I'm in the SDP. Still, I promise to write to the Town Hall for nomination papers. 'There's no kitty as yet,' she says, 'and I wouldn't want to do any of that meeting people. I'd be no good at that. The secretaries can do that (you get expenses). But I'd be very good at voting, better than they are, probably.'

May 1983 Miss S. asks me to witness her signature on the nomination form. 'I'm signing,' she says: 'Are you witnessing?' She has approached various nuns to be her nominees. 'One sister I know would have signed but I haven't seen her for some years and she's got rather confused in the interim. I don't know what I'll do about leaflets. It would have to be an economy job, I couldn't run to the expense. Maybe I'll just write my manifesto on the pavement, that goes round like wildfire.'

May 1983 Miss S. has received her nomination papers. 'What should describe myself as?' she asks through the window slit. 'I thought Elderly Spinster possibly. It also says Title. Well my title is' – and she laughs one of her rare laughs – 'Mrs Shepherd. That's what some people call me out of politeness. And I don't deny it. Mother Teresa always says she's married to God. I could say I was married to the Good Shepherd, and that's what it's to do with, Parliament, looking after the flock. When I'm elected, do you think I shall have to live in Downing Street or could I run things from the van?'

26

I speak to her later in the day and the nomination business is beginning to get her down. 'Do you know anything about the Act of 1974? It refers to disqualifications under it. Anyway, it's all giving me a headache. I think there may be another election soon after this one, so it'll have been good preparation anyway.'

June 1984 Miss S. has been looking in *Exchange and Mart* again and has answered an advert for a white Morris Minor. 'It's the kind of car I'm used to – or I used to be used to. I feel the need to be mobile.' I raise the matter of a licence and insurance, which she always treats as tiresome formalities. 'What you don't understand is that I am insured. I am insured in heaven.' She claims that since she has been insured in heaven there has not been a scratch on the van. I point out that this is less to do with the celestial insurance than with the fact that the van is parked the whole time in my garden. She concedes that when she was on the road the van did used to get the occasional knock. 'Somebody came up behind me once and scratched the van. I wanted him to pay something, half-a-crown I think it was. He wouldn't.'

October 1984 Some new staircarpet fitted today. Spotting the old carpet being thrown out, Miss S. says it would be just the thing to put on the roof of the van to deaden the sound of rain. This exchange comes just as I am leaving for work, but I say that I do not want the van festooned with bits of old carpet – it looks bad enough as it is. When I come back in the evening I find half the carpet remnants slung over the roof. I ask Miss S. who has put them there as she can't have done it herself. 'A friend,' she says mysteriously. 'A well-wisher.' Enraged I pull down a token piece but the majority of it stays put.

April 1985 Miss S. has written to Mrs Thatcher applying for a post in 'the Ministry of Transport advisory, to do with drink and driving and that'. She also shows me the text of a letter she is proposing to send to the Argentinian Embassy on behalf of General Galtieri. 'What he doesn't understand is that Mrs Thatcher isn't the Iron Lady. It's me.'

To Someone in Charge of Argentina. 19 April 1985

Dear Sir,

I am writing to help mercy towards the poor general who led your forces in the war actually as a person of true knowledge more than might be. I was concerned with Justice, Love and, in a manner of speaking, I was in the war, as it were, shaking hands with your then leader, welcoming him in spirit (it may have been to do with love of Catholic education for Malvinas for instance) greatly meaning kindly negotiators etc . . . but I fear that he may have thought it was Mrs Thatcher welcoming him in that way and it may hence have unduly influenced him.

Therefore I beg you to have mercy on him indeed. Let him go, re-instate him, if feasible. You may read publicly this letter if you wish to explain mercy etc.

      I remain.

            Yours truly

               A Member of the Fidelis Party

                 (Servants of Justice)

P.S. Others may have contributed to undue influence also.

P.P.S. Possibly without realising it.

      Translate into Argentinian if you shd wish.

Sometime in 1980 Miss S. acquired a car, but before she'd managed to get more than a jaunt or two in it ('It's a real goer!') it was stolen and later found stripped and abandoned in the basement of the council flats in Maiden Lane. I went to collect what was left ('though the police may require it for evidence, possibly') and found that even in the short time she'd had the Mini she'd managed to stuff it with the usual quota of plastic bags, kitchen rolls and old blankets, all plentifully doused in talcum powder. When she got a Reliant Robin in 1984 it was much the same, a second wardrobe as much as a second car. Miss Shepherd could afford to splash out on these vehicles because being parked in the garden meant that she had a permanent address, and so qualified for full social security and its various allowances. Since her only outgoings were on food, she was able to put by something and had an account in the Halifax and quite a few savings certificates. Indeed I heard people passing say, 'You know she's a millionaire,' the inference being no one in their right mind would let her live there if she weren't.

Her Reliant saw more action than the Mini and she would tootle off in it on a Sunday morning, park on Primrose Hill ('The air is better') and even got as far as Hounslow. More often than not, though, she was happy (and I think she was happy then) just to sit in the Reliant and rev the engine. However, since she generally chose to do this first thing on Sunday morning, it didn't endear her to the neighbours. Besides, what she described as 'a lifetime with motors' had failed to teach her that revving a car does not charge the battery, so that when it regularly ran down I had to take it out and re-charge it, knowing full well this would just mean more revving. ('No,' she insisted, 'I may be going to Cornwall next week, possibly.') This re-charging of the battery wasn't really the issue: I was just ashamed to be seen delving under the bonnet of such a joke car.

March 1987 The nuns up the road, or as Miss S. always refers to them 'the sisters', have taken to doing some of her shopping.

One of them leaves a bag on the back step of the van this morning. There are the inevitable ginger nuts and several packets of sanitary towels. I can see these would be difficult articles for her to ask me to get, though to ask a nun to get them would seem quite hard for her too. They form some part of her elaborate toilet arrangements and are occasionally to be seen laid drying across the soup-encrusted electric ring. As the postman says this morning, 'the smell sometimes knocks you back a bit.'

May 1987 Miss S. wants to spread a blanket over the roof (in addition to the bit of carpet) in order to deaden the sound of the rain. I point out that within a few weeks it will be dank and disgusting. 'No,' she says. 'Weather-beaten.'

She has put a Conservative poster in the side window of the van. The only person who can see it is me.

This morning she was sitting at the open door of the van and as I edge by she chucks out an empty packet of Ariel. The blanket hanging over the pushchair is covered in washing powder. 'Have you spilt it?' I enquire. 'No,' she says crossly, irritated at having to explain the obvious. 'That's washing powder. When it rains the blanket will get washed.' As I work at my table now I can see her bending over the pushchair, picking at bits of soap flakes and re-distributing them over the blanket. No rain is at the moment forecast.

June 1987 Miss S. has persuaded the Social Services to allocate her a wheelchair, though what she's really set her heart on is the electric version.

Miss S.: That boy over the road has one, why not me?

Me: He can't walk.

Miss S.: How does he know? He hasn't tried.

Me: Miss Shepherd, he has Spina Bifida.

Miss S.: Well, I was round-shouldered as a child. That may not be serious now but it was quite serious then. I've gone through two wars, an infant in the first and not on full rations, in the ambulances in the second, besides being failed by the ATS. Why should old people be disregarded?

Thwarted in her ambition for a powered chair Miss S. compensated by acquiring (I never found out where from) a second wheelchair ('in case the other conks out, possibly'). The full inventory of her wheeled vehicles now read: one van; one Reliant Robin; two wheelchairs; one folding wheely; one folding (two-seater) wheely. Now and again I would thin out the wheelies by smuggling one onto a skip. She would put down this disappearance to children (never a favourite) and the number would shortly be made up by yet another wheely from Reg's junk stall. Miss S. never mastered the technique of self-propulsion in the wheelchair because she refused to use the inner handwheel ('I can't be doing with all that silliness'). Instead, she preferred to punt herself along with two walking-sticks, looking in the process rather like a skier on the flat. Eventually I had to remove the handwheel ('The extra weight affects my health').

July 1987   Miss S. (bright green visor, purple skirt, brown cardigan, turquoise fluorescent ankle socks) punts her way out through the gate in the wheelchair in a complicated manoeuvre which would be much simplified did she just push the chair out, as well she can. A passer-by takes pity on her and she is whisked down to the market. Except not quite whisked, because the

31

journey is made more difficult than need be by Miss S.'s refusal to take her feet off the ground, so the Good Samaritan finds himself pushing a wheelchair continually slurred and braked by these large trailing carpet-slippered feet. Her legs are so thin now the feet are as slack and flat as those of a camel.

Still, there will be one moment to relish on this, as on all these journeys. When she has been pushed back from the market she will tell (and it is tell, there is never any thanks) whoever is pushing the chair to leave her opposite the gate but on the crown of the road. Then, when she thinks no one is looking, she lifts her feet, pushes herself off and freewheels the few yards down to the gate. The look on her face is one of pure pleasure.

October 1987 I have been filming abroad. 'When you were in Yugoslavia,' asks Miss S., 'did you come across the Virgin Mary?' 'No,' I say, 'I don't think so.' 'Oh, well, she's appearing there. She's been appearing there every day for several years.' It's as if I've missed the major tourist attraction.

January 1988 I ask Miss S. if it was her birthday yesterday. She agrees guardedly. 'So you're 77.' 'Yes. How did you know?' 'I saw it once when you filled out the census form.' I give her a bottle of whisky, explaining that it's just to rub on. 'Oh. Thank you.' Pause. 'Mr Bennett. Don't tell anybody.' 'About the whisky?' 'No. About my birthday.' Pause. 'Mr Bennett.' 'Yes?' 'About the whisky either.'

March 1988 'I've been doing a bit of spring cleaning,' says Miss S. kneeling in front of a Kienholz-like tableau of filth and decay.

32

She says she has been discussing the possibility of a bungalow with the social worker to which she would be prepared to contribute 'a few hundred or so'. It's possible that the bungalow might be made of asbestos, 'but I could wear a mask. I wouldn't mind that and of course it would be much better from the fire point of view.' Hands in mittens made from old socks. A sanitary towel drying over the ring and a glossy leaflet from the Halifax offering 'fabulous investment opportunities'.

April 1988 Miss S. asks me to get Tom M. to take a photograph of her for her new bus-pass. 'That would make a comedy, you know. Sitting on a bus and your bus-pass out of date. You could make a fortune out of that with very little work involved, possibly. I was a born tragedian,' she says, 'or a comedian possibly. One or the other anyway. But I didn't realise it at the time. Big feet.' She pushes out her red unstockinged ankles. 'Big hands.' The fingers stained brown. 'Tall. People trip over me. That's comedy. I wish they didn't, of course. I'd like it easier but there it is. I'm not suggesting you do it,' she says hastily, feeling perhaps she's come too near self-revelation, 'only it might make people laugh.' All of this is said with a straight face and no hint of a smile, sitting in the wheelchair with her hands pressed between her knees and her baseball cap on.

May 1988 Miss S. sits in her wheelchair in the road, paintpot in hand, dabbing at the bodywork of the Reliant which she will shortly enter, start and rev for a contented half-hour before switching off and paddling down the road in her wheelchair. She has been nattering at Tom M. to mend the clutch, but there are conditions: it mustn't be on Sunday, which is the feast of St Peter

33

and St Paul and a day of obligation. Nor can it be the following Sunday apparently, through the Feast of the Assumption falling on the Monday and being transferred back to the previous day.

Amid all the chaos of her life and now, I think, more or less incontinent she trips with fanatical precision through this liturgical minefield.

September 1988 Miss S. has started thinking about a flat again, though not the one the Council offered her a few years ago. This time she has her eye on something much closer to home. My home. We had been talking in the hall and I left her sitting on the step in the hall while I came back to work. This is often what happens, me sitting at my table, wanting to get on, Miss S. sitting outside rambling. This time she goes on talking about the flat, soliloquising almost, but knowing that I can hear: 'It need only be a little flat, even a room possibly. Of course, I can't manage stairs, so it would have to be on the ground floor. Though I'd pay to have a lift put in.' (Louder.) 'And the lift wouldn't be wasted. They'd have it for their old age. And they'll have to be thinking about their old age quite soon.' The tone of it is somehow familiar from years ago. Then I realise it's like one of the meant-to-be-overheard soliloquies of Richmal Crompton's William.

Her outfit this morning: orange skirt, made out of three or four large dusters; a striped blue satin jacket; a green headscarf, blue eyeshield topped off by a khaki peaked cap with a skull-and-crossbones badge and Rambo across the peak.

February 1989 Miss S.'s religion is an odd mixture of traditional faith and a belief in the power of positive thinking. This morning, as ever, the Reliant battery is running low and she asks me to fix it. The usual argument takes place:

Me: Well, of course it's run down. It will run down unless you run the car. Revving up doesn't charge it. The wheels have to go round.

Miss S.: Stop talking like that. This car is not the same. There are miracles. There is faith. Negative thoughts don't help. *She presses the starter again and it coughs weakly.* There, you see. The devil's heard you. You shouldn't say negative things.

The interior of the van now indescribable.

March 1989 Miss S. sits in the wheelchair trying to open the sneck of the gate with her walking-stick. She tries it with one end, then reverses the stick and tries with the other. Sitting at my table, trying to work, I watch her idly, much as one would watch an ant trying to get round some obstacle. Now she bangs on the gate to attract the attention of a passer-by. Now she is wailing. Banging and wailing. I go out. She stops wailing, and explains she has her washing to do. As I manoeuvre her through the gate I ask her if she's fit to go. Yes, only she will need help. I explain that I can't push her there. (Why can't I?) No, she doesn't want that. Would I just push her as far as the corner? I do so. Would I just push her a bit further? I explain that I can't take her to the launderette. (And anyway there is no launderette any more so which launderette is she going to?) Eventually feeling like Fletcher Christian (only not Christian) abandoning Captain Bligh, I leave her in the wheelchair outside Mary H.'s. Someone will come along. I would be more ashamed if I did not feel, even when she is poorly, that she knows exactly what she's about.

March 1989 There is a thin layer of talcum powder around the back door of the van and odd bits of screwed up tissues smeared with what may or may not be shit, though there is no doubt about the main item of litter which is a stained incontinence pad. My method of retrieving these items would not be unfamiliar at Sellafield. I don rubber gloves, put each hand inside a plastic bag as an additional protection, then, having swept the faecal artefacts together, gingerly pick them up and put them in the bin. 'Those aren't all my rubbish' comes a voice from the van. 'Some of them blow in under the gate.'

April 1989 Miss S. has asked me to telephone the Social Services and I tell her that a social worker will be calling. 'What time?' 'I don't know. But you're not going to be out. You haven't been out for a week.' 'I might be. Miracles do happen. Besides, she may not be able to talk to me. I may not be at the door end of the van. I might be at the other end.' 'So she can talk to you there.' 'And what if I'm in the middle?'

Miss C. thinks her heart is failing. She calls her Mary. I find this strange, though it is of course her name.

April 1989 A staple of Miss S.'s shopping list these days is sherbet lemons. I have a stock of them in the house but she insists I invest in yet more so that a perpetual supply of sherbet lemons may never be in doubt. 'I'm on them now. I don't want to have to go off them.' I ask her if she would like a cup of coffee.

'Well, I wouldn't want you to go to all that trouble. I'll just have half a cup.'

Towards the end of her life Miss S. was befriended by an ex-nurse who lived locally. She put me in touch with a day centre who agreed to take Miss Shepherd in, give her a bath and a medical examination and even a bed in a single room where she

36

could stay if she wanted. In retrospect I see I should have done something on the same lines years before, except that it was only when age and illness had weakened Miss Shepherd that she would accept such help. Even now it was not easy.

April 27 1989 A red ambulance calls to take Miss S. to the day centre. Miss B. talks to her for a while in the van, gradually coaxing her out and into the wheelchair, shit streaks over her swollen feet, a piece of toilet roll clinging to one scaly ankle. 'And if I don't like it,' she keeps asking, 'can I come back?' I reassure her but looking at the inside of the van and trying to cope with the stench, I find it hard to see how she can go on living here much longer. Once she sees the room they are offering her, the bath, the clean sheets, I can't imagine her wanting to come back. And indeed she makes more fuss than usual about locking the van door, which suggests she accepts that she may not be returning. I note how, with none of my distaste, the ambulance driver bends over her as he puts her on the hoist, his careful rearrangement of her greasy clothing, pulling her skirt down over her knees in the interest of modesty. The chair goes on the hoist and slowly she rises and comes into view above the level of the garden wall and is wheeled into the ambulance. There is a certain distinction about her as she leaves, a Dorothy Hodgkin of vagabonds, a derelict Nobel Prize-winner, the heavy folds of her grimy face set in a kind of resigned satisfaction. She may even be enjoying herself.

When she has gone I walk round the van noting the occasions of our old battles: the carpet tiles she managed to smuggle onto the roof, the blanket strapped on to muffle the sound of the rain, the black bags under the van stuffed with her old clothes –

37

sites of skirmishes all of which I'd lost. Now I imagine her bathed and bandaged and cleanly clothed and starting a new life. I even see myself visiting and taking flowers.

This fantasy rapidly fades when around 2.30 Miss S. reappears, washed and in clean clothes, it's true, and with a long pair of white hospital socks over her shrunken legs, but obviously very pleased to be back. She has a telephone number where her new friends can be contacted and she gives it to me. 'They can be reached,' she says, 'any time, even over the holiday. They're on a long-distance bleep.'

As I am leaving for the theatre, she bangs on the door of the van with her stick. I open the door. She is lying wrapped in clean white sheets on a quilt laid over all the accumulated filth and rubbish of the van. She is still worrying that I will have her taken to hospital. I tell her there's no question of it and that she can stay as long as she wants. I close the door, but there is another bang and I reassure her again. Once more I close the door but she bangs again. 'Mr Bennett.' I have to strain to hear. 'I'm sorry the van's in such a state. I haven't been able to do any spring cleaning.'

April 28 I am working at my table when I see Miss B. arrive with a pile of clean clothes for Miss Shepherd which must have been washed for her at the day centre yesterday. Miss B. knocks at the door of the van, then opens it, looks inside and – something nobody has ever done before – gets in. It's only a moment before she comes out and I know what has happened before she rings the bell. We go back to the van where Miss Shepherd is dead, lying on her left side, flesh cold, face gaunt, the neck stretched out as if for the block and a bee buzzing round her body.

38

It is a beautiful day with the garden glittering in the sunshine, strong shadows by the nettles and bluebells out under the wall, and I remember how in her occasional moments of contemplation she would sit in the wheelchair and gaze at the garden. I am filled with remorse for my harsh conduct towards her, though I know at the same time that it was not harsh. But still I never quite believed or chose to believe she was as ill as she was and I regret too all the questions I never asked her. Not that she would have answered them. I have a strong impulse to stand at the gate and tell anyone who passes.

Miss B. meanwhile goes off and returns with a nice doctor from St Pancras who seems scarcely out of her teens. She gets into the van, takes the pulse in Miss S.'s outstretched neck, checks her with a stethoscope and, to save an autopsy, certifies death as from heart failure. Then comes the priest to bless her before she is taken to the funeral parlour and he, too, gets into the van, the third person to do so this morning and all of them without distaste or ado in what to me seem three small acts of heroism. Stooping over the body, his bright white hair brushing the top of the van, the priest murmurs an inaudible prayer and makes a cross on Miss S.'s hands and head. Then they all go off and I come inside to wait for the undertakers.

I have been sitting at my table for ten minutes before I realise that the undertakers have been here all the time, and that death nowadays comes (or goes) in a grey Ford transit van that is standing outside the gate. There are three undertakers, two young and burly, the third older and more experienced, a sergeant as it were and two corporals. They bring out a rough greypainted coffin, like a prop a conjuror might use, and making no comment on the surely extraordinary circumstances in which they find it, put a sheet of white plastic bin-liner over the body and manhandle it into their magic box, where it falls with a bit of a thud. Across the road, office workers stroll down from the Piano Factory for their lunch, but nobody stops or even looks much, and the Asian woman who has to wait while the box is carried over the pavement and put in the (other) van doesn't give it a backward glance.

Later I go round to the undertakers to arrange the funeral, and the manager apologises for their response when I had originally phoned. A woman had answered, saying: 'What exactly is it you want?' Not thinking callers rang undertakers with a great variety of requests, I was nonplussed. Then she said briskly: 'Do you want someone taking away?' The undertaker explains that her seemingly unhelpful manner was because she thought my call wasn't genuine. 'We get so many hoaxes these days. I've often gone to collect a corpse only to have it open the door.'

9 May Miss Shepherd's funeral is at Our Lady of Hal, the Catholic church round the corner. The service has been slotted into the ten o'clock Mass so that, in addition to a contingent of neighbours, the congregation includes what I take to be regulars: the fat little man in thick glasses and trainers who hobbles along to the church every day from Arlington House; several nuns, among them the 99-year-old sister who was in charge when Miss S. was briefly a novice; a woman in a green straw hat like an upturned plant pot who eats toffees throughout; and another lady who plays the harmonium in tan slacks and a tea-cosy wig. The server, a middle-aged man with white hair, doesn't wear a surplice, just ordinary clothes with an open-necked shirt, and but for knowing all the sacred drill, might have been roped

40

in from the group on the corner outside The Good Mixer. The priest is a young Irish boy with a big red peasant face and sandy hair and he, too, stripped of his cream-coloured cassock, could be wielding a pneumatic drill in the roadworks outside. I keep thinking about these characters during the terrible service and it reinforces what I have always known: that I could never be a Catholic because I'm such a snob and that the biggest sacrifice Newman made when he turned his back on the C of E was the social one.

Yet kindness abounds. In front of us is a thin old man who knows the service backwards, and seeing we have no prayer-books, he lays down his own on top of his copy of the *Sun*, goes back up the aisle to fetch us some and hands them round, all the time saying the responses without faltering. The first hymn is Newman's 'Lead Kindly Light' which I try and sing, while making no attempt at the second hymn, which is 'Kum Ba Ya'. The priest turns out to have a good strong voice, though its tone is more suited to 'Kum Ba Ya' than Newman and J. B. Dykes. The service itself is wet and wandering, even more so than the current Anglican equivalent, though occasionally one catches in the watered-down language a distant echo of 1662. Now, though, arrives the bit I dread, the celebration of fellowship, which always reminded me of the warm-up Ned Sherrin insisted on inflicting on the studio audience before *Not so much a programme*, when everyone had to shake hands with their neighbour. But again the nice man who fetched us the prayer-books shames me when he turns round without any fuss or embarrassment and smilingly shakes my hand. Then it is the Mass proper, the priest distributing the wafers to the 99-year-old nun and the lady with the plant pot on her head, as Miss S. lies in her coffin at his elbow.

41

Finally there is another hymn, this one by the (to me) unknown hymnodist Kevin Norton, who's obviously reworked it from his unsuccessful entry for the Eurovision Song Contest; and with the young priest acting as lead singer and the congregation a rather subdued backing group, Miss Shepherd is carried out.

The neighbours, who are not quite mourners, wait on the pavement outside as the coffin is hoisted onto the hearse. 'A cut above her previous vehicle,' remarks Colin H.; and comedy persists when the car accompanying the hearse to the cemetery refuses to start. It's a familiar scene and one which I've played many times, with Miss S. waiting inside her vehicle as well-wishers lift the bonnet, fetch leads and give it a jump start. Except this time she's dead.

Only A. and I and Clare, the ex-nurse who lately befriended Miss S., accompany the body, swept over Hampstead Heath at a less than funereal pace, down Bishop's Avenue and up to the St Pancras Cemetery, green and lush this warm sunny day. We drive beyond the scattered woods to the furthest edge where stand long lines of new gravestones, mostly in black polished granite. Appropriately, in view of her lifelong love of the car, Miss S. is being buried within sight and sound of the North Circular Road, one carriageway the other side of the hedge with juggernauts drowning the words of the priest as he commits the body to the earth. He gives us each a go with his little plastic bottle of holy water, we throw some soil into the grave, and then everybody leaves me to whatever solitary thoughts I might have, which are not many, before we are driven back to Camden Town, life reasserted when the undertaker drops us handily outside Sainsbury's.

42

In the interval between Miss Shepherd's death and her funeral ten days later I found out more about her life than I had in twenty years. She had indeed driven ambulances during the war and was either blown up or narrowly escaped death when a bomb exploded nearby. I'm not sure that her eccentricity can be put down to this any more than to the legend, mentioned by one of the nuns, that it was the death of her fiancé in this incident that 'tipped her over'. It would be comforting to think that it is love, or the death of it, that unbalances the mind, but I think her early attempts to become a nun and her repeated failures ('too argumentative,' one of the sisters said) point to a personality that must already have been quite awkward when she was a girl. After the war she spent some time in mental hospitals but regularly absconded, finally remaining at large long enough to establish her competence to live unsupervised.

The turning-point in her life came when through no fault of hers a motorcyclist crashed into the side of her van. If her other vans were any guide, this one too would only have been insured in heaven so it's not surprising she left the scene of the accident ('skedaddled', she would have said) without giving her name or address. The motorcyclist subsequently died so that, while blameless in the accident, by leaving the scene of it she had committed a criminal offence. The Police mounted a search for her. Having already changed her first name when she became a novice, now under very different circumstances she changed her second and, calling herself Shepherd, made her way back to Camden Town and the vicinity of the convent where she had taken her vows. And though in the years to come she had little to do with the nuns or they with her, she was never to stray far from the convent for the rest of her life.

All this I learned in those last few days. It was as if she had been a character in Dickens whose history has to be revealed and her secrets told in the general setting-to-rights before the happy ever after, though all that this amounted to was that at long last I could bring my car into the garden to stand now where the van stood all those years.

The Lady in the Van first appeared in the *London Review of Books*.
If you would like to subscribe to the paper send
your name and address to:

London Review of Books
LRB, FREEPOST
Tavistock House South, Tavistock Square
London WC1H 9BR